Spread the Word

Spread the Word

A Woman's Workshop on Luke

With Helps for Leaders

Evelyn Bence

Lamplighter Books Grand Rapids, Michigan
Zondervan Publishing House

Spread the Word: A Woman's Workshop on Luke

This is a Lamplighter Book
Published by the Zondervan Publishing House
1415 Lake Drive, S.E., Grand Rapids, Michigan 49506

Library of Congress Cataloging in Publication Data

Bence, Evelyn, 1952–
  Spread the word.
  "This is a Lamplighter Book"—T.p. verso.
  Bibliography: p.
  1. Bible. N.T. Luke—Text-books. I. Title.
BS2595.5.B46 1984   226'.406   84–11809
ISBN 0-310-44781-X

Unless otherwise indicated, the Scripture text used is that of the New International Version (North American Edition), copyright 1978 by the International Bible Society. Used by permission.

Edited by Larry J. Nyberg

Printed in the United States of America

84 85 86 87 88 89 / 10 9 8 7 6 5 4 3 2 1

CONTENTS

ACKNOWLEDGMENTS

Hearty thanks to my sister Alice Davidson who was willing to approach her Bible study group with "Let's experiment," and to the members of her Otego, New York, circle who studied from inconvenient photocopies of a rough manuscript and offered invaluable suggestions:

April Farina	Leslie Peters
Claire Joyce	Ferrissa Sheldon
Phyllis Koepke	Linda Urben
Leona McMorris	Sherry Zerbe
Bette Miller	

Thank you, Sandra Adams, for your encouraging input—for your life.

HOW TO USE THIS STUDY GUIDE

Spread the Word is designed for group discussion of material that has first been individually and privately studied and thought through.

The Gospel of Luke is a long portion of Scripture to cover in thirteen lessons. To make the most of your time and study the book as thoroughly as possible, try following these few suggestions:

1. Early in the week, as part of your private devotions, read the entire lesson's passage. Then as you answer the questions, read the verses again in the indicated smaller segments.

2. The lesson discussion (not allowing for reading the Scripture aloud) should take one and one-quarter hours. If your group's schedule allows for more time, you will want to read the passage aloud in your weekly meeting as you progress through the questions. If your schedule does not

allow for additional time, each member should reread the Scripture directly before coming to the discussion.

3. Regular members of the group might take turns leading the discussion. That way you will share both the burden and the benefits of the extra preparation involved in guiding the lesson. The helps for leaders have been placed in the back of this students' manual to make shared leadership as easy as possible; you will have no extra book to pass around from week to week.

Although a leader should not dominate the study, she should be careful to keep the lesson flowing and to prevent tangents from diverting the conversation from the issues at hand. But any group's most important leader is the Holy Spirit, who is eager to guide the thoughts and words of His women as they hear the Word of the Lord.

THE GOSPEL OF LUKE

The Gospel of Luke has long been considered one of the most beautiful books ever written. When Luke, a physician, followed the Spirit's leading and put pen to paper, the words flowed gracefully and the story of Jesus' life unfolded clearly.

Luke's gospel is unique on several accounts and thus is particularly interesting to study. Although little is known about Luke, it is generally agreed that, unlike the other gospel writers, he was a Gentile. Theophilus, the man to whom this account was written, was also a Gentile, and probably a man holding some noteworthy position. One theme keeps running through Luke's letter to him: Jesus' coming was for the benefit of *all* people, not just the Jews.

Luke's concern for all people includes an unusual sensitivity to women. He presents them as having a significant part in Jesus' ministry. Perhaps Luke was from Macedonia, where women were generally held in higher esteem than in first-century Jewish culture. The poor, the sick—those who suffered on every account—were "taken up" by Jesus, as portrayed by Luke.

Luke's gospel can best be studied as a whole. He is very conscious of time; a story—more than a story, God's plan of redemption—slowly unfolds. Mysteries become apparent only when it is time for them to be revealed. Like a good storyteller, Luke gives hints of what Jesus is all about, but holds the punch till the end of the book.

As you study, keep in mind that the story will not be completed until lesson 13.

1

GOD GIVES, WE RESPOND

Luke 1:1–2:40

Promises. Are they words worth our total trust? Should we hold back a part of ourselves, cross our fingers, and hope they will be kept? Should we dig in our heels and say, "I'm from Missouri. I won't believe until I see the end results"?

Wait a minute, you may say. You haven't given me enough information. It all depends on who makes the promises— whether or not he or she has power, authority, credentials, a good reputation.

Of course. And who is more capable of fulfilling His word than God? But, even so, do we trust that He will "come through"? And when He does, how do we respond?

Let's look at some promises God made to His people as a whole and to individuals—Zechariah, Elizabeth, Mary, Joseph, the shepherds, Simeon, and Anna. How did each respond to His Word and His gifts, His promises and His answers? What can we learn from them?

Read Luke 1:1–38.

1. Why should we trust Luke's account of life in first-century Israel (vv. 1–4)?

   Because he researched all info. He rechecked everything. He was a physician and a man of detail. He wanted to be sure everything he wrote was factual

2. What credentials for foretelling truth did Gabriel give Zechariah (vv. 19–20)? Gabriel said: I am Gabriel and I stand in the presence of God and I have been sent to speak to you & to tell you this good news.

3. What promises of good gifts did Gabriel make? To Zechariah? That John would be a joy & delight to him & Elizabeth. That John would bring back many of the people of Israel to God. John will be filled w/ the Holy Spirit at birth

   To Mary? That her son would be the son of the most high. He would reign over the house of Jacob forever and his Kingdom would never end.

4. In what ways was Gabriel's message to Zechariah similar to his message to Mary?

   _____

   _____

   _____

   _____

5. What differences do you see in the responses of the two individuals?

Mary completely Accepted what Gabriel told her " I am the Lord's Servant—may it be to me as you have said" Zechariah questioned asking "How Can I be Sure of this" and was struck Dumb until after John was born.

6. Read Genesis 18:10–14 and then reread Luke 1:37. Surely Zechariah, a priest, knew the Old Testament Scriptures; he must have known the words of God to Abraham and Sarah who had been in a similar situation. Why is it so easy to forget the message of verse 37 when *we* are in the "impossible" situation and are promised a miracle?

_____

_____

_____

Read 1:39–80.

7. List characteristics of Mary and Elizabeth you desire to emulate. Next to each, determine how you might strive this week to follow their example.

Mary   This week

_____   _____

_____   _____

_____   _____

_____   _____

Elizabeth   This week

_____   _____

_____   _____

_____   _____

_____   _____

8. Carefully read Zechariah's prophecy (vv. 67–79). For what was he praising God?

_____

_____

List the events he foretold.

_____

_____

_____

9. Describe the change that came over Zechariah in the months covered in this chapter.

_____

_____

What accounts for the differences?

_____

_____

Read 2:1–7.

10. Place yourself in Mary's position. What would have been your natural reaction to the circumstances of your delivery not "working out" as you might have hoped?

_____

_____

_____

Read 2:8–20.

11. List in chronological order the responses of the shepherds to the angel's appearance and news—that they would *see* the fulfillment of a promise made to the Jewish people centuries earlier.

_____

_____

_____

_____

12. Which of the shepherds' reactions seems most exemplary and why?

_____

_____

_____

Read 2:21–40.

13. For Simeon the sight of the baby Jesus signaled the end of a long personal wait. God gave Simeon and Anna a special inner (no angels here) knowledge of Jesus' imminent arrival. What do you learn from them about "waiting on God"?

_____

_____

14. Summarize what the angel and the various prophecies in this lesson's passage said about who Jesus was and what He would do.

_____

_____

_____

_____

15. Summarize what you have learned about believing in and acting on the promises of God.

_____

_____

_____

Key Verses:

"For nothing is impossible with God" (1:37).

"Praise be to the Lord, the God of Israel, because he has come and has redeemed his people" (1:68).

2

TWO MEN, TWO MISSIONS

Luke 2:41–4:44; 7:18–35

"Repent."

How many cartoonists have made light of modern-day prophets who wage solitary wars against sin?

Such pleas for repentance are nothing new, but are as old as the Scriptures themselves. And the people who delivered those pleas, then as now, were often unusual, even unsettling, individuals. Does God use only people who are neatly defined and able to be put in labeled boxes? Does He fulfill our expectations of how He should work? Life as shown in Luke 3–4 is full of surprises, as is life in our contemporary world.

Read Luke 2:41–52.

1. What familial ties did Jesus break or establish here?

_____

_____

_____

_____

2. How or why could Jesus have been a puzzlement to Mary, who had been told by an angel who He was?

_____

_____

Read 3:1–22.

3. John may have been a prime candidate for a course in winning friends and influencing people. Describe his method of delivery.

_____

_____

_____

4. What did John demand and of whom did he demand it?

_____

_____

_____

5. What is the difference between the purposes of John's work and of Jesus' work?

_____

_____

_____

_____

6. What signs did the baptism of Jesus give and to whom?

_____

_____

_____

Has God given you any signs of His presence? Have you given the world any signs? What would they be?

_____

_____

_____

Skim 3:23–37.

7. Matthew's geneology of Jesus starts with Abraham (see Matthew 1:1–17); Luke's goes back to the beginning of life. Why are these extra generations important to the overall message of the Gospel of Luke?

_____

_____

_____

Why are they important for us readers?

_____

_____

Read Luke 4.

8. Each of the cited wilderness situations tempted Jesus to misuse the power He clearly had. What light do these temptations shed on our tendency to want to "prove" our righteousness? Our competence? Our authority?

_____

_____

_____

_____

_____

9. What unseen power is mentioned repeatedly in reference to Jesus' actions?

_____

10. What reputations was Jesus gathering?

_____

_____

11. Jesus was intent on "staying the course." How would the memory of the preceding victories and signs of God's presence have helped Him throughout His daily ministry?

_____

_____

How have such memories affected your Christian walk?

_____

_____

Read 7:18–35.

12. In specific terms, compare Jesus' style of life with John's.

_____

_____

_____

Compare their physical ministries.

_____

_____

_____

13. How could someone who had been so sure of Jesus' coming be questioning Jesus' identity? What about John's past assurances?

_____

_____

_____

_____

14. By what standard should we evaluate a person's ministry (vv. 33–35)?

_____

_____

_____

15. Within the biblical guidelines, we must listen daily for God's word to us. He has given us all the same general framework of Christianity. The specifics of the particular mission He has for each of us, however, are an individual matter. Write a sentence description of what you see as your life's specific mission up to this point.

_____

_____

_____

In closing, pray, asking God for specific direction. Does He want you to "stay the course"? Does He want you to stay in your profession, but clean up your act? Does He want you to make drastic changes? Ask that He confirm His will in your life, as well as in the lives of the other members of your group.

Key Verses:

"I baptize you with water. But one more powerful than I will come" (3:16).

"Wisdom is proved right by all her children" (7:35).

3

YOU DON'T KNOW ALL THE ANSWERS? THEN FOLLOW ME

Luke 5:1–6:49

"Follow me."

Whether spoken tenderly in your ear by a loved one, firmly by the police officer whose car sits ahead of yours, or pleasantly by a tour guide, these two words call for action.

You can ignore them, but you can't, in truth, claim to be following when you are sitting still, revving your motor, or marking time.

When walking through Palestine Jesus sought out some of His followers, whereas others sought after Him like children following a houseguest who is known to carry a pocketful of candy.

No matter which group one belonged to, one thing was clear: Following Jesus called for God-ward movement.

Let's see what that means for us, Jesus' modern disciples.

Background Information

Pharisees: A Jewish sect in New Testament times. They believed in the resurrection of the dead (as opposed to the Sadducees who did not). Not only were they fanatical about keeping the Law of Moses, they added to it a rigid code of personal behavior which was based on tradition. They are now looked upon as having been the ultimate spiritual hypocrites.

Tax collectors: Jewish people who worked for the governing Romans. They were considered traitors to their own race and were further despised because they were generally dishonest, collecting more money than Rome required and pocketing the difference.

Read Luke 5:1–11, 27–32; 6:12–16.

1. What did Jesus command, and how did the following people respond?

	Command	Response
Peter:	_____	_____
	_____	_____
Levi (thought to be Matthew):	_____	_____
	_____	_____

2. What effect would their responses have on their futures?

_____

_____

_____

3. What did Peter see in himself? In Jesus (v. 8)?

_____

_____

What does Jesus' "Don't be afraid" offer Peter? What does it offer us?

_____

_____

_____

Note 5:31–32.

4. If Jesus were recruiting His followers today, for whom would He look and where?

_____

_____

_____

Read 5:12–26, 33–39.

5. What actions preceded each of these healings?

Leper:

_____

_____

Paralytic:

_____

_____

6. Whose faith and action was responsible for the paralytic's wholeness?

_____

7. How might we sometimes carry the responsibility of another's salvation or healing?

_____

_____

8. To receive God's forgiveness and healing, what must we acknowledge?

_____

9. In verses 33–39, what light is shed on people's inclination to work to patch up the holes in their old ways of life rather than to seek new life—in Christ?

_____

_____

_____

Read 6:1–11.

10. Think of Jesus' illustration of the old wineskins and the new wineskins. What do they suggest for today?

_____

_____

Read 6:17–42.

11. To whom is this sermon directed?

_____

How does this make it clear that Jesus was not just adding more legalistic rules to the already long list of pharisaical dos and don'ts for gaining salvation?

_____

_____

_____

12. List three points from this sermon that you have the most difficulty with.

_____

_____

_____

_____

Read 6:43–49.

13. Jesus' analogies are logical, yet demanding—even condemning. What connection did Jesus make between a follower's heart, actions, and words?

_____

_____

_____

_____

14. Summarize chapters 5 and 6 by defining what it means to follow Jesus.

_____

_____

_____

_____

_____

Pause for individual meditation and private prayer, acknowledging the needs in your life. Christ *is* the answer—the Savior, the Healer, the Peacegiver, the Strengthgiver. Go through your list in question 12; admit your shortcomings, confess your heart's desire to follow Christ, ask Him for forgiveness and sustaining strength.

Key Verses:

"I have not come to call the righteous, but sinners to repentance" (5:32).

"Why do you call me, 'Lord, Lord,' and do not do what I say?" (6:46).

4

REAL-LIFE FAITH, HOPE, AND LOVE

Luke 7:1–17; 7:36–8:56

When I was a child I learned a song I have not yet forgotten, "God can do anything, but fail."

As a six-year-old it was so easy to believe, but worry and doubt have a way of creeping in along with age.

In 1 Corinthians 13 the apostle Paul says that faith, hope and love abide forever. Here in Luke 7 and 8, faith in God's power, hope in His deliverance, and love for Him who loves us are played out in real-life encounters between Jesus and various followers.

The disciples, who in earlier chapters left their jobs to follow Jesus, were not necessarily the people who knew the most about these qualities.

Let's take a closer look at how faith, hope, and love work together to effect healing and wonders beyond expectation.

Background Information

Centurion: A Roman army commander, obviously a Gentile. Even though this particular centurion was God-fearing and benevolent, his mere presence was a reminder of foreign rule.

Dinner Party: Uninvited strangers sometimes entered a dining area and watched the reclining, shoeless guests.

Read Luke 7:1–10.

1. What character qualities make this centurion noteworthy?

   _____

   _____

   _____

2. The centurion was accustomed to having words produce actions; what then was so unusual about his expectations of Jesus?

   _____

   _____

   _____

3. In your own words, define *faith*. Compare this with a dictionary definition.

   _____

   _____

   _____

   _____

Read 7:11–17, 36–50.

4. Consider all three stories. What persons show love and to whom?

Centurion's story:

_____

_____

Widow's story:

_____

_____

Anointing:

_____

_____

5. Why did Jesus forgive the prostitute's sins?

_____

_____

6. What connection is established here between faith and love?

_____

_____

_____

Read 8:1–18.

7. What credit does Luke give to Jesus' women disciples?

_____

_____

What does this imply about their commitment to love?

_____

_____

8. List all the hindrances to spiritual growth noted in the explanation of the parable of the sower.

_____

_____

_____

What is expected of the mature Christian?

_____

_____

9. Relate verses 16–18 to the parable of the sower. Note Luke's emphasis on how we hear.

_____

_____

_____

Read 8:19–25.

10. On what footing was Jesus putting those who practice what they correctly hear?

_____

11. The disciples did call upon Jesus, so what basis did Jesus have for chastising them?

_____

_____

What does this say about the "fruits" of faith?

_____

_____

Read 8:26–39.

12. How did the ex-demoniac want to show Jesus his love and gratitude? What did Jesus require of him?

_____

_____

Read 8:40–56.

13. Compare the hemorrhaging woman's unspoken faith to the disciples' "Master, Master . . ." in verse 24.

_____

_____

_____

14. What hope do these healings give women today?

_____

_____

15. Over what forces did Jesus show His power?

_____

How does the scope of His influence show His love for us?

_____

_____

16. List four ways you can, this week, live out your faith in and love for Him.

_____

_____

_____

_____

Key Verses:

"Your faith has saved you (healed you); go in peace" (7:50; 8:48).

"No one lights a lamp and hides it in a jar or puts it under a bed. Instead, he puts it on a stand, so that those who come in can see the light" (8:16).

5

BUT I DON'T UNDERSTAND

Luke 9:1–11:13

"But I don't understand."

The disciples could very well have said the words daily as they followed Jesus from town to town. As best they knew how, they tried to help Him, but they never seemed to see things in the same light as He.

Jesus was full of mystery. Sometimes He seemed terribly concerned about explaining what was going on and other times He spoke cryptically.

In this week's lesson He first refers to His suffering and death. We, knowing the end of the story, can see what Jesus was talking about, but to the disciples it was a puzzle. They still had no real idea what they'd got themselves into. That wouldn't come until life after Jesus' death.

Read Luke 9:1–6.

1. For what purpose were the twelve apostles being trained?

_____

_____

Read 9:7–36.

2. In what ways was Herod's question of verse 9 answered in these subsequent incidents?

The feeding:

_____

Peter's confession:

_____

The transfiguration:

_____

3. How do verses 23–27, directed to Jesus' followers, help explain who He was and what He was about?

_____

_____

_____

_____

_____

4. In terms of gains and losses, Luke tells us who we should be (vv. 23–27). What areas of your life do you hold onto for dear life? (Have you ever thought something like: "He *can't* take *that* from me"?)

_____

_____

_____

_____

Imagine loosening your grasp on that piece of life and placing it in God's hand. What would happen?

_____

_____

What does this release have to do with faith, hope, and love?

_____

_____

_____

Read 9:37–57.

5. List the ways in which the disciples "mess up" or fail to understand Jesus' message or tactics. If they had been properly "tuned in" to Jesus, how might they have responded?

	What happened	What might have happened
9:33	_____	_____
	_____	_____
9:40–41	_____	_____
	_____	_____
9:44–45	_____	_____
	_____	_____
9:46–48	_____	_____
	_____	_____

9:49–50 _____   _____

_____   _____

9:51–56 _____   _____

_____   _____

6. How can Luke 9:50 be reconciled with Jesus' words in Luke 11:23?

_____

_____

_____

7. The disciples' actions seem so typically human. What insight do they give into our passion for doing things our own way?

_____

_____

_____

8. How long did Jesus put up with His disciples?

_____

Read 9:57–62; 10:25–37.

9. What priorities do these passages place on a follower's life?

_____

_____

_____

10. How would "Who is your neighbor?" be answered in modern terms?

_____

_____

Read 10:1–24; 11:1–13.

11. With what are Jesus' followers to be concerned?

_____

_____

12. Previously Jesus seems to have chastized people for not hearing. In 9:45 and 10:21–22 He seems to say that God hides the truth from some people. Then in 11:5–13 He assures that if we seek we will find. How can these points be reconciled with each other?

_____

_____

_____

_____

Read 10:38–42.

13. Again, Jesus gets very close to home in His demands. What did Martha not understand?

_____

_____

14. It seems to us that the disciples should have understood more of the truth about Jesus and His work; after all, they had Him physically at their side. But we all "see through a glass darkly." What resources do we now have at our disposal to help us understand truths that the disciples might not have understood?

_____

_____

How can we make best use of those resources so that we can best understand?

_____

_____

Key Verses:

" 'But what about you?' he asked. 'Who do you say I am?' Peter answered, 'The Christ of God' " (9:20).

"For whoever wants to save his life will lose it, but whoever loses his life for me will save it" (9:24).

"Ask and it will be given to you; seek and you will find, knock and it will be opened to you" (11:9).

6

OH, BE CAREFUL!

Luke 11:14—13:9

Jesus never let His disciples rest on their past faith and actions. He continually warned them to be careful, to guard themselves against sin. Yet He also encouraged them to rest in and on Him, not on their strivings or their righteousness. It sounds as if He was asking them to balance on a tightrope, and He was.

Let's get filled in on the details.

Background Information

Unmarked graves: Hidden, unacknowledged containers of "poison" and death.

Read Luke 11:14–36.

1. To prevent its return, what must accompany the ridding of evil?

_____

_____

In practical terms how can we accomplish this?

_____

_____

_____

2. What type of signs did Jesus refuse to give and what kind did He give freely?

_____

_____

_____

_____

Read 11:37–54.

3. Summarize the core of each of Jesus' six complaints against the Pharisees and law experts (vv. 42–52).

a. _____

_____

b. _____

_____

c. _____

_____

d. _____

_____

e. _____

_____

f. _____

_____

In each case what confession and turn about would have changed Jesus' woe to a blessing?

a. _____

_____

b. _____

_____

c. _____

_____

d. _____

_____

e. _____

_____

f. _____

_____

4. Perhaps one of Jesus' woes gave you a twinge of guilt. Rewrite it with contemporary imagery. What personal changes would effect a canceling of this woe?

_____

_____

_____

_____

Read 12:1–34.

5. In two verses (5, 7) Jesus told His disciples both to fear and not to be afraid. What differentiation did He make between these two kinds of fear?

_____

_____

_____

6. What does being "rich toward God" involve (v. 21)? Be specific in your answer.

_____

_____

_____

_____

7. List circumstances about which Jesus says not to worry.

_____

_____

8. What does worry accomplish?

_____

9. How and under what conditions will our needs be met?

_____

_____

10. Imagine yourself at this time tomorrow. Overnight your earthly possessions have been lost in a fire and you have no insurance coverage on which to fall back. What state of mind would you be in? Relate your answer to verse 34.

_____

_____

_____

_____

Read 12:35–53.

11. For what are we hearers responsible (vv. 35–48)?

_____

_____

12. Relate an incident where Jesus might bring division rather than the unity we would naturally expect of Him.

_____

_____

Read 12:54–13:9.

13. How eager is God to bring listeners to repentance?

_____

_____

14. Review the lesson by listing what you, a follower of Jesus, are to guard against or be careful of.

_____

_____

_____

_____

15. Determine where your heart and therefore your treasure is. What is your heart's passion? What measures could you take this week to move your passion Godward?

_____

_____

_____

_____

Key Verses:

"But seek his kingdom, and these things will be given to you as well" (12:31).

"Where your treasure is, there your heart will be also" (12:34).

7

HEAR YE, HEAR YE

Luke 13:10–14:35

"All to Jesus I surrender." Without much thought Carolyn joined her congregation in singing the familiar gospel song. As the last "I surrender all" drifted out of her mouth, she realized she didn't have any idea what she was talking about.

She desired to please Christ, but she felt so small and inadequate. She wanted to live in God's will, but what *did* it mean?

Let's look further into Luke to learn what Jesus said in the form of paradoxes—seeming contradictions—that would help Carolyn see what the song meant in terms of life on Monday morning.

Read 13:10–17.

1. What was Jesus' attitude toward suffering?

What responses did this healing elicit?

_____

_____

Read 13:18–21.

2. Several lessons are taught by the parables of the mustard seed and the yeast. What do you think they say about the kingdom of God or about God's grace?

_____

_____

_____

3. In your own experience, what small seed or leaven has grown into what larger grace?

_____

_____

_____

Read 13:22–35.

4. Where was Jesus intent on going?

_____

5. The Jews thought their Jewishness and consciousness of the Law would guarantee their salvation. Who did Jesus say will be saved?

_____

6. Jesus described Himself in terms of a female image (v. 34). What does this say about Him?

_____

_____

Read 14:1–14.

7. Recognition. Who doesn't want it? What kind of recognition did Jesus acknowledge as worthwhile?

_____

_____

8. Imagine yourself consistently following Jesus' direction and always taking the least honorable place. But instead of being invited to the high place, you never are acknowledged. What would be your prayer? What should be your prayer?

_____

_____

_____

9. What motives did Jesus require behind our generosity and hospitality?

_____

_____

10. "But I've had them to dinner twice and I've never even seen the inside of their house." Is it hard not to keep accounts? Who else is keeping account of what?

_____

_____

Read 14:15–24.

11. What do the three excuses have in common with each other? What different issue does each deal with?

_____

_____

_____

_____

_____

12. Put yourself in the place of the host. How tolerant was he
of such excuses?

_____

Read 14:25–35.

13. In verse 26, the word *hate* can be understood best in
terms of detachment. Review the portions of Luke you
have previously studied. What was Jesus' reaction to His
family? Discuss whether or not Jesus' practice and
preaching seems irresponsible.

_____

_____

_____

14. What was Jesus saying about conversions that smack of
"Don't read the fine print, just sign on the dotted line"?
What does the "fine print" of following Christ involve?

_____

_____

15. What four uses are made of salt?

_____

_____

_____

_____

16. What spiritual application can be made of each use?

_____

_____

What happens when we lose our saltiness?

_____

_____

17. As an overview of the lesson, skim the entire passage and note the context of Jesus' images involving size and place, such as large, small, narrow, first, last.

_____

_____

_____

_____

_____

18. Write a sentence that summarizes these teachings as they relate to your life and any changes Christ is demanding of you.

_____

_____

_____

Key Verses:

"Woman, you are set free from your infirmity" (13:12).

"Make every effort to enter through the narrow door" (13:24).

"You will be repaid at the resurrection of the righteous" (14:14).

"Any of you who does not give up everything he has cannot be my disciple" (14:33).

8

LOST OR FOUND

Luke 15:1−16:31

"I once was lost, but now am found." The wayward son in this week's lesson would have had every reason to sing whole-heartedly this line of "Amazing Grace."

"I was blind but now I see" could have been sung by the rich man who wished Lazarus would come comfort his hellish agony. But for him, grace seemed out of reach.

With open arms God offers grace to all. He wants all His sheep safe inside His fold, but not all will enter in.

Let's dig further and discover some reasons.

Read Luke 15:1−32.

1. What importance did Jesus put on the salvation of the lost?

_____

_____

2. In each of the three stories, who initiated the reunion?

Sheep: _____

Coin: _____

Son: _____

3. Compare the answers of question two to our relationship with God. Who finds whom? In your own life, what have you sensed to be the case?

_____

_____

4. What brought the lost son to his senses?

_____

5. What did he expect from his father and what did he receive?

_____

_____

_____

6. What do these parables say about any loved ones you have who may be lost? What is your part in their being found?

_____

_____

7. Look at the two brothers. List the character traits (good and bad) you see in each.

Older	Younger
_____	_____
_____	_____

_____   _____

8. How do you identify with either/both son(s)?

_____

_____

9. List the character traits you see in the father.

_____

_____

10. How will God respond to you, His child?

_____

Read 16:1–18.

11. How might our use of money bear on our welcome into the kingdom? What light does verse 15 shed on your answer?

_____

_____

_____

12. What connection did Jesus make between earthly responsibility and spiritual responsibility?

_____

_____

13. Has Jesus made following God more or less demanding than it was in Old Testament times? (See Matthew 5:17–48.) Explain your answer.

_____

_____

_____

14. Janet has carefully been noting Jesus' teaching that we should be detached from our families. She has decided this is justification for her leaving her husband. Discuss this in light of 16:18.

_____

_____

Read 16:19–31.

15. How did the rich man's view of life change when he was on the other side of death?

_____

_____

16. What do we need in order to find God's truth?

_____

17. Review chapters 15 and 16. For what did Jesus show patience; over what did He show intolerance?

_____

_____

What accounts for the difference in His attitudes?

_____

_____

Close your lesson with short conversational prayers, thanking God for His grace shown in His seeking the lost, for His grace shown in providing us with the Scriptures—the guideposts of our daily search for His will.

Key Verses:

"There is rejoicing in the presence of the angels of God over one sinner who repents" (15:10).

"Whoever can be trusted with very little can also be trusted with much, and whoever is dishonest with very little will also be dishonest with much" (16:10).

"No servant can serve two masters. . . . You cannot serve both God and Money" (16:13).

9

MAKING CHOICES

Luke 17:1–18:34

Being a Christian is often compared to being a spouse. A commitment is firmly made, but if the commitment isn't backed up with daily choices that show continued love, the joy of a rich relationship quickly dissolves. Depending on yesterday's signs of affection doesn't work for very long. Jesus knew this when He said, "If you love me, keep my commandments."

In Luke 17 and 18 Jesus is still teaching His followers what that means—on a daily basis.

Read Luke 17:1–10.

1. How might we lead someone else into sin?

_____

_____

2. How might we "watch ourselves" (v. 3)?

_____

_____

3. Discuss the following example: Clara read verses 1–3 and suddenly realized that her father, who had set a bad example, was responsible for her chronic ill-temper. What a relief; if she could blame him, she wasn't responsible for her sin.

_____

_____

_____

4. Why is forgiveness such a difficult but important lesson? (Note Luke 11:4.)

_____

_____

5. Verses 5–10 were probably not direct responses to verses 3–4. In placing them in this order, what was Luke saying?

_____

_____

Read 17:11–19.

6. List the various choices the thankful leper made on the day he was healed. What effect did they have on his life?

_____

_____

_____

7. In what ways can we follow his example?

_____

_____

8. Why would Luke—and Jesus—point out the thankful leper's nationality? Why is it significant now?

_____

_____

Read 17:20–37.

9. How will we recognize the coming kingdom?

_____

_____

10. In this passage, what choices does Jesus ask us to make?

_____

_____

11. Reread verses 31–35. At Jesus' second coming, who will choose whom?

_____

12. What is said here about individual accountability?

_____

Read 18:1–17.

13. What should characterize our approach to God in prayer? What choices do these approaches involve?

_____

_____

_____

14. Discuss Wendy's response to verses 9–14. She finished reading them and said, "I'm really glad I'm not like the Pharisee."

_____

Read 18:18–34.

15. What choices were put before the rich ruler? What reward was at the further end of either choice? Relate verses 29–30 to Jesus' sacrifice in verse 32.

_____

_____

_____

16. Daily we choose. And spiritually we reap the reward of our choices. List three choices (either important or relatively insignificant) you have made in the past week. In light of eternal values, would you repeat each decision? What changes would you make if yesterday were tomorrow?

_____

_____

_____

Key Verses:

"The apostles said to the Lord, 'Increase our faith!' " (17:5).

"Anyone who will not receive the kingdom of God like a little child will never enter it" (18:17).

"No one who has left home or wife or brothers or parents or children for the sake of the kingdom of God will fail to receive many times as much in this age and, in the age to come, eternal life" (18:29–30).

10

ACKNOWLEDGING THE LORD

Luke 18:35–20:26; 20:41–21:4

Knowing what was ahead of Him, Jesus walked into Jerusalem without flinching. He was truly a king—in control, even when appearances seemed to indicate otherwise.

Although they still did not know what His kingship or kingdom was all about, some people in Jerusalem acknowledged Him as their king and lord. Others schemed over ways to get rid of Him.

If we acknowledge Jesus as Lord over our lives, what will it require? What protection will we receive in return?

Read Luke 18:35–19:10.

1. What characterizes both of these seekers?

_____

_____

2. What is so desirable about the transformations Jesus effects?

_____

_____

3. What complaints did the people around Jesus air? Why did they seem never to learn? Put yourself in their shoes. Would you have "caught on" by now?

_____

_____

_____

Read 19:11–27.

4. What were the actions of the three servants and what were their respective rewards?

_____

_____

_____

5. In verse 26, what nouns might appropriately fit after the first "has"?

_____

_____

6. List three "investments" a healthy fear of God might motivate you to make. Discuss how you might help each other go about making them.

_____

_____

_____

Read 19:28–48.

7.a. List the various groups that acknowledged Jesus as Lord.

_____

_____

b. Compare verse 27 with verse 44. With what does Jesus seem concerned?

_____

8. What motivated the crowd in their praise? Is this a legitimate cause for praise?

_____

_____

9. What elements of praise are described and what part do they have in your life?

_____

_____

10. What emotions are expressed in this passage? Which ones do you feel are justified and why?

_____

_____

_____

11. What should be the place of each of the above emotions in your life? What steps can you take that would lead you toward this ideal goal?

_____

_____

_____

Read 20:1–26, 41–47.

12. What characteristics of humanity does the parable of the tenants portray?

_____

_____

What characteristics of God?

_____

_____

13. What is the answer to Jesus' question in verse 17?

_____

14. What was the basis for Jesus' authority?

_____

15. How did Jesus respond to those He knew were trying to trick Him?

_____

Read 21:1–4.

16. What comment was Jesus making on the quality and quantity of our commitment to His lordship?

_____

_____

17. Review the whole lesson. When a person acknowledges Jesus' lordship over her life, what actions and attitudes result?

_____

_____

_____

_____

Key Verses:

"I tell you, . . . if they keep quiet, the stones will cry out" (19:40).

"The stone the builders rejected has become the capstone" (20:17).

11

WHAT LIES AHEAD?

Luke 20:27–40; 21:5–22:34

Remembrances—letters, cards, mementos, gifts—connect us to those we love but who are not physically with us. They remind us that the past existed and of the events it contained. (How easy it is to forget.) They fill the present with life and with joy, with assurances that we are not isolated and alone, and with strength.

In Luke 21 and 22, Jesus talks of the future in terms that are somewhat bleak, yet He gives a remembrance so we will not forget the past—His life and the victory of His death.

Background Information

Sadducees: A small but powerful and wealthy Jewish group who cooperated with the foreign Roman government to protect their aristocratic privileges. They revered highly only the five books of Moses; they did not believe in life after death nor did they look forward to the coming of the

Messiah. Here the Sadducees ask Jesus a question they think is unanswerable. They reason that such an absurd question disproves the existence of an afterlife.

Read Luke 20:27–40.

1. List what Jesus says we can eventually expect.

   _____

   _____

2. How does God view the death of the righteous?

   _____

   _____

Read 21:5–38.

3. What meaning do you see behind Jesus' immediate answer in verse 8 to the disciples' request for a sign?

   _____

   _____

4. Summarize what Jesus told His followers they could expect to happen before the end of the age.

   _____

   To the nations:

   _____

   To Jerusalem:

   _____

   To families:

   _____

To believers:

_____

To nature:

_____

5. What must we guard ourselves against and how?

Guard Against	Method
_____	_____
_____	_____

6. Who will help the faithful and how?

_____

7. What should be our goal throughout these predicted hard times?

_____

Read 22:1–34.

8. For what did Judas betray Jesus and how did this show he did not understand Jesus' kingdom?

_____

_____

9. Why might Jesus have chosen such physical and ordinary elements and actions by which we are to remember Him?

_____

_____

10. In what ways might our commemoration of this Last Supper strengthen us in times of trial?

_____

_____

11. Consider verses 23–24. In what ways did the disciples show they did not know themselves or each other very well.

_____

_____

_____

12. How might our lack of self-knowledge increase our faith in God (or what effect might this insight have on our relationship with God)?

_____

_____

13. How does a Christian gain respect or authority?

_____

14. Reread verses 31–32. What characters are in this short scenario and who was in control?

_____

_____

15. When might we be in the midst of similar spiritual battles? How might we ultimately remain true rather than give in, as did Judas?

_____

_____

Key Verses.

"Heaven and earth will pass away, but my words will never pass away" (21:33).

"Be always on the watch, and pray that you may be able to escape all that is about to happen, and that you may be able to stand before the Son of Man" (21:36).

"Do this in remembrance of me" (22:19).

"But I am among you as one who serves" (22:27).

12

WERE YOU THERE?

Luke 22:35–23:43

Good intentions. At least eleven of the twelve disciples were full of them, but under pressure they "fell apart." Jesus was left to walk His valley alone.

Despite the disciples' unfaithfulness, Jesus remained faithful to them. Luke describes His love and commitment in bold contrast to theirs.

His calm inner strength and costly obedience to His father are an example for us, His modern-day disciples, to follow.

Read Luke 22:35–62.

1. Why should the disciples have been praying?

_____

2. Jesus could have asked His disciples to encircle Him in prayer. Surely they then would have stayed awake. What might His praying alone have taught His disciples? What

does it teach us?

_____

_____

3. Who hasn't fallen asleep while praying? How can we guard ourselves against "slipping off"?

_____

4. What makes this one–sentence prayer of Jesus such a perfect example of how we should approach God (v. 42)?

_____

_____

5. How easy (or difficult) is doing God's will? What "rewards" compensate for any unpleasantness?

_____

_____

6. Compare Jesus' concern for self-defense with His concern for His enemies.

_____

_____

7. Review verses 35–38 in light of verses 47–53. To what could Jesus have been referring in verses 36–37?

_____

_____

8. What makes Peter's story different from Judas's?

_____

_____

_____

9. What does Peter's example show us about repentance in the life of a believer?

_____

_____

Read 22:63–23:25.

10. With what was Jesus charged and what was the immediate reason for His death sentence? What was the larger reason behind these occurrences?

_____

_____

_____

11. Why was Pilate not without guilt?

_____

_____

Read 23:26–43.

12. Luke is the only Evangelist who mentions the women in verses 28–31. What comfort, if any, can be gleaned from these verses?

_____

_____

13. "If you perform a magic trick for me, I'll believe You, Jesus." Why does this attitude not work?

_____

14. What actions of Jesus prove His humility?

_____

_____

15. Consider how often your sacrifice or suffering for someone else occasions false humility—a martyr complex. Discuss Jesus' attitudes and how He can help you incorporate them into your life.

_____

_____

_____

16. Review the various scenes of this story. How did each person or group sin and how did Jesus react?

	Their Sin	Jesus' Reaction
Sleeping disciples:		
Judas:		
Captors:		
Peter:		
Accuser:		
Criminals:		

17. How great was Jesus' love and to what extent did He forgive? How is this important to you—today?

_____

_____

_____

Key Verses:

"Father, if you are willing, take this cup from me; yet not my will, but yours be done" (22:42).

"Father, forgive them, for they do not know what they are doing" (23:34).

13

SPREAD THE WORD!

Luke 23:44–24:53

The apostle Paul, quoting an Old Testament prophecy, put the story of the Resurrection in a nutshell: "Death has been swallowed up in victory" (1 Corinthians 15:54).

Jesus, in rising, ushered us into a new age of hope. He won our battle against sin for us. He threw open the doors of the kingdom, so all who believed could freely enter in.

Let's take a look at the sequence of events and share with the disciples their new joy and their new job.

Background Information

The curtain of the temple: The curtain that hid the presence of God (the Holy of Holies) from the rest of the temple and from the people. Only the high priest could enter the Holy of Holies and only one day a year, the Day of Atonement, when his actions atoned for the sins of the people.

The sixth hour: Noon.

Read Luke 23:44–56.

1. What do the darkness and the tearing of the curtain symbolize for us?

_____

_____

_____

2. What reactions did Jesus' death prompt?

_____

_____

3. If verse 56 were the end of the story, what would have been the point of Jesus' life?

_____

_____

Read Luke 24.

4. What bondage does "He is risen" break? What hope does this give us?

_____

_____

5. In light of last week's passage, what do Peter's presence and action say about him (vv. 1–12)?

_____

_____

6. What did it take to get the following people to believe:

The women?

_____

Peter?

_____

The traveling two?

_____

The disciples?

_____

Read John 20:29.

7. On what is your own belief based?

_____

_____

_____

8. What correlation can be drawn between familiarity with a teaching and belief in it?

_____

_____

9. "We had hoped . . ." (v. 21). In what daily situations are we guilty of similar shortsightedness?

_____

_____

10. In a sentence or two summarize what Jesus explains about Himself in Luke 24.

_____

_____

_____

_____

11. Also read Acts 1:1–11 and Matthew 28:16–20. What are we to preach and in what power?

_____

_____

12. In Luke 24, through what stages do the disciples' attitudes progress?

_____

_____

13. Why such joy at a farewell (see vv. 52–53)?

_____

_____

14. What or who makes us joyful?

_____

15. What part can you play in carrying out the great commission?

_____

_____

16. Think back over the whole Gospel of Luke. What new understanding have you heard?

_____

_____

_____

17. What changes in your actions, words, or attitudes has your hearing prompted?

_____

_____

_____

18. What effect has/does/will your hearing have on the lives of those around you?

_____

_____

Close the study in prayer, asking that the Holy Spirit help you become an instrument through which He will make the story of Jesus' life and redemption clear to others.

Key Verses:

"Why do you look for the living among the dead? He is not here; he has risen!" (24:5–6).

"I am going to send you what my Father has promised" (24:49).

"Then they worshiped him and returned to Jerusalem with great joy" (24:52).

LEADERS HELPS

1 / GOD GIVES, WE RESPOND

4. Note that in each case the angel sensed and allayed fear before relaying his message. If we are fearful, can we really be open to hearing objectively? Discuss the details of the angel's messages: He told the mission of each baby, and, directly or indirectly, he told each parent-to-be of the coming of the other's child.

5. On first glance it is not easy to see why Zechariah was reprimanded for unbelief whereas Mary was given a simple explanation to her question. Didn't they both ask, "How?" But examine their responses further. Zechariah seems to have asked for proof in a skeptical "show me" attitude, whereas Mary asked no questions about whether or not the angel's word would come to pass, but rather asked only an innocent "By what means?"

6. Angelic visits have never been everyday occurrences. God's promises to us are most likely spoken through Scriptures and the small voice of the Holy Spirit.

8. A promise had been fulfilled. Is there any life-changer more powerful than the assurance that comes when God makes the impossible possible for *you* ?

Verse 67 clearly states that Zechariah was filled with the Holy Spirit and was given His words and power to speak of the future.

10. How easy it is for us to forget that God's hand is at work even when our physical surroundings are less than comfortable. How easy to forget the miracles that brought us into our present situation.

12. Of course the answers to this question will vary. You might want to stress the shepherds' spreading of the word and point out that they acted immediately on the angel's message.

For further discussion:

1. Mary's song (1:46–55) is patterned after Hannah's praise for her long-awaited son, Samuel. Quickly skim 1 Samuel 2:1–10, comparing the vocabulary and images of the two women's songs. What do your observations imply about the place of Scripture in Mary's life?

2. In relation to question 7, discuss the following line from Martin Luther's hymn "A Mighty Fortress": "Did we in our own strength confide, Our striving would be losing."

2 / TWO MEN, TWO MISSIONS

1. A Jewish boy first went to Passover in Jerusalem when he was twelve years old. This trip was Jesus' initiation into adulthood. This also seems to be the first time Jesus was aware of or at least referred to His uniqueness, saying God, not Joseph, was His father, thus establishing loyalties.

2. Review the details Mary was given by the angel or through words of prophecy (Lesson 1). Pretty skimpy. A lot of images which vaguely describe the end results of Jesus' coming, but not much insight into what Mary could expect on a daily basis; her life would prove to be full of surprises. Is this true of our own Christian walk? In this study we will learn principles, we will learn that circumstances work together for good, but we will see that the working out of the details comes as surprises, as tests of faith, as personal lessons and victories.

3, 4. John the Baptist is described in greater physical detail in Mark 1:6. He did not exactly try to "fit in" with either the secular or the religious community. He told the Jews, proud of and secure in their heritage, to share with the lowly, despised poor; he told the tax collectors not to quit their corrupt profession, but to keep their jobs while cleaning up their acts; he told the soldiers to use their power justly and to be content. John threatened even his most powerful target, accusing Herod of adultery. For this John was imprisoned and eventually killed.

6. Jesus, being without sin (1 Peter 2:22), did not need to get right before God and take part in this visible sign of repentance (baptism), but in the eyes of the people He may have needed to identify Himself with those who were contrite; He may have needed to give the people a sign, showing them which side He was on. A second sign was the Holy Spirit, seen in the form of a dove. A third sign was a heavenly voice, reminding Jesus of His identity.

7. Luke and Theophilus were Gentiles, as are most contemporary Christians. Christ came for the benefit of *all* people, as we all are descendants of Adam and, in that physical sense, children of God.

8. Satan asked Jesus to prove Himself. Jesus maintained that He would not perform magic tricks in order to show someone who He was. (This happened again when Jesus was prodded to prove that He was the Son of God by taking Himself down from the cross.) His relationship to God was based on God's approval, not on the approval of Satan.

11. We often disregard Jesus' being fully human. He was tempted not only in the wilderness, but just as we are. Surely He needed to keep reminding Himself of God's presence within Him, just as we do.

13. When first-century Jews talked of wanting a Messiah, they thought in terms of political deliverance. Their people wanted a king of their own who would bring in the kingdom—here on earth. Jesus might not have been what John was expecting. John needed to remember to "hold onto" what God had given him in the past.

14. I like to think of verse 35 as meaning "Truth is truth." This verse might be closely aligned with "By their fruit you will recognize them" (Matthew 7:16, 20). Jesus here describes two totally different types of ministries; both are of God, yet both are ridiculed for being extreme and not the ordinary. Is there a place for Salvation Army street meetings as well as sophisticated spiritual retreat work?

For further discussion:

1. Discuss whether or not John had a good perspective on his place in God's plan. (In this discussion you might refer to John 3:30.)

2a. In relation to question 14 ask: Where can Jesus or the Spirit of God be found?

b. Think back over the past few weeks. In what unexpected places have you found God at work?

3 / YOU DON'T KNOW ALL THE ANSWERS? THEN FOLLOW ME

3. Peter's acknowledgment of his sin allowed him to recognize Jesus as holy and as his Savior. In saying, "Don't be afraid," Jesus was telling Peter his sins were not counted against him.

4. It was the church leaders who, depending on their own righteousness, didn't follow Jesus. He called fishermen (a respectable but not lofty profession), tax collectors, and the sick and maimed. You might discuss whether Jesus would be recognized by the church as the Messiah if He hadn't come to first-century Palestine, but came to our country today.

6, 7. Luke acknowledges the faith (and subsequent actions) of the friends of the paralyzed man. My pastor frequently repeats his pet phrase: "There's no such thing as solo Christianity." God does answer our prayers, which are often prayers on behalf of our loved ones. Our actions and faith on their behalf can be a channel of grace through which God works, by which God brings them to Him, and which God blesses.

You might want to read the following quote by Ladislaus Boros to spur discussion. Do you agree with his observation?

"As a concrete expression of his love for God, man has nothing but his neighbour . . . . By his very nature he is dependent on brotherly love as a condition which makes his faith possible."

—Living in Hope

8. The accusing Pharisees refused to acknowledge any sin or need. In this passage those whom Jesus helped or forgave saw in Jesus the answer to their lack. They acknowledged they were not whole and they saw the answers to their void or problems as being outside themselves—in the grace and mercy of Jesus.

For further discussion:

1. Regarding question 9, discuss this observation by Joseph Fitzmyer:

"The new does not just repair the old; rather, the old must give way."

—The Gospel According to Luke I-IX
(Anchor Bible)

4 / REAL-LIFE FAITH, HOPE, AND LOVE

5, 6. Verse 47 comments on the prostitute's love; verse 50 refers to her faith. The nature of love demands that any declaration of it be backed up or proven with actions. Does a woman whose husband mistreats her really believe that he loves her? Needs her, maybe, but perfectly loves her? Can love of and faith in God be separated?

7. Luke gives a great deal of attention to the women who were touched by Jesus' life. He does not dismiss them, but acknowledges them as active followers. Their love for Jesus was shown tangibly by their "support." They traveled with Him and gave to Him, thanking Him for their deliverance from sin. Note the descriptions of the women. Their love must have been strong to have such a diversified group (the wife of a political leader alongside an ex-demoniac).

9. It may be easy for us to hide from each other our true spiritual conditions. But verse 17 (repeated again in 12:12) makes it clear that all will eventually be brought to light. A convert's initial enthusiasm (the joy of verse 13) is not necessarily an indication of his or her hearing abilities; the true test is in perseverance. Note the encouragement of verse 18 (repeated in 19:26)—whoever has been given insight will be given more.

13. Remember, a menstruating woman was considered "unclean." Mark 5:26 says she had suffered greatly under the care of doctors and had spent all she had on them, yet continued to grow worse. This woman had lived twelve years in disgrace grown into despair. Jesus not only gave her health, but called her "daughter" and gave her peace. Her expectant looking to Jesus healed her, without her even telling Him of her need. His love and power cured. Why? Because He knew her heart. He also knew the hearts of His disciples. He saw their fear and, no doubt, the mistrust in their eyes.

For further discussion:

1. Discuss the implications of the following: Sally was brought up in a Christian home and always lived what she considered a "good" life. She found the conversation between Jesus and Simon the Pharisee (7:41–47) thought-provoking. Maybe she should have an affair or commit a series of "big" sins so she would receive a "big" forgiveness and be made more capable of love.

In your discussion you might point out that Scripture builds on other Scripture. Review other followers of Jesus studied earlier in Luke. Was Mary (Jesus' mother) a reformed "grave" sinner? Did it seem the fishermen were "down and outers"? The centurion? On the other hand, were the "clean cut" Pharisees truly righteous? In Jesus' eyes is one sin less serious than a great number of sins, or many sins worse than a few? Was He speaking in terms of measurements because Simon was thinking in those terms? Consider Romans 6:1.

5 / BUT I DON'T UNDERSTAND

General Background

Why might Jesus have made such a mystery of His mission?

Especially early in His ministry, it seems as if the timing for the release of such knowledge was premature. Remember, the Jews were looking for a Messiah who would physically deliver them from the Romans. In the wilderness Jesus had resisted the temptation to use His power wrongly, but could He have wanted to keep Himself from excessive crowd pressure to fulfill their expectations? Could He have known that too much early knowledge of the plan would have somehow thwarted it?

Jesus knew who He was, and in time those whose hearts were open would also know. These three years of ministry were years of preparation for those close to Him. After the Resurrection His veiled words of the past would become clear (it was just a matter of time) and then the crowds would know who had been among them and what His life and death had accomplished.

The nature of Jesus' work called for it to be carried out without the aid of a publicist.

3. Jesus asks nothing of His followers that He does not require of Himself. Although it sounds as if He is describing what He requires of us, He is also describing what He will do in bringing about our redemption.

4. The gain that comes from losing is something not teachable, only learnable. Only when we have taken the step of release, the step of faith that trusts that God desires His best for us, can we know the truth of this verse. It is the core of what God requires of followers. The disciples had to "lose" their fishing, the sick their charitable status, the rich their security, the proud their positions, the worriers their fussing. Most of the disciples actually lost life itself, all to gain the kingdom which is life with a capital L.

6. The disciples were told to assume that those who were not against them were for them implying that we mortals do not know each other's hearts. Jesus, knowing our hearts, can rightly judge that we who are not for Him are against Him. Each of us is responsible for our own choice of being against or for, rather than worrying about others. Leon Morris points out:

> When a man sees what the kingdom means he must be either for it or against it.
>
> —*The Gospel According to St. Luke*
> (Tyndale New Testament Commentaries)

12. Jesus' seeming contradiction could be as simple as: He withholds the truth from those who truly do not seek it.

14. We have the complete Scriptures and therefore the whole story; the enlightening Holy Spirit.

For further discussion:

1. As an overview of the lesson, discuss the Old Testament verse: "As the heavens are higher than the earth, so are my ways higher than your ways and my thoughts than your thoughts" (Isaiah 55:9).

6 / OH, BE CAREFUL!

1. Exorcising evil and leaving one's house clean seems not to be enough. To ward off reinvasion of the evil, a house must be filled with good.

3c. They hid corruption and uncleanness so well, no one even knew that they were, in effect, poison—hiding death.

7. Consider the insight of verse 11 along with verses 22–34. The Holy Spirit will prod us with ideas and answers to our legitimate predicaments. Jesus' mention of "little faith" implies that faith is an important ingredient to the meeting of our needs, and, of course, seeking Christ and His truth is the central issue.

12. Truth, goodness, and love easily threaten those who feel conviction but who love their sin and do not want to give it up. Jesus' coming seems to have heightened rather than alleviated the age-old struggle of good versus evil.

Besides legitimate divisions caused by the Gospel, there are illegitimate divisions. Work done in Jesus' name but not of Him has divided people and nations for centuries.

For further discussion:

1. Should we actually go out and sell our homes and give away our incomes to prove God's faithfulness in meeting our needs?

2. Should a woman's heart (and therefore her treasure) be her husband and children?

3. Does Luke 12:34 work if reversed? (Where your heart is, there will your treasure be also.)

7 / HEAR YE, HEAR YE

General Background

Keep in mind that Jesus knew His destination and His physical fate. His followers did not, but expected that when He got to Jerusalem He would establish His kingship. The teachings of this lesson were, in a sense, warnings of what they were following Him into.

1. It doesn't seem that this woman's life was in danger, yet Jesus saw the dissolving of her infirmity as more important than the letter of the law. Jesus was full of mercy. He seemed so intent on alleviating suffering that He did so without this woman even asking to be healed.

2. A few suggestions:

Mustard seed: A small beginning can cause a great ending. (A small step of faith, a small yearning for God, a small witness can lead to a miraculous cleansing from sin, a miraculous grace.)

Lest you bury a seed, it will not grow. (To gain life you must lose it.)

The kingdom (the tree) is big enough to house many different birds of the air—many varieties of believers. (See Ezekiel 31:6.) Yeast: A little truth effects a great change. (Individuals grow more and more Christlike; individuals can influence larger groups to be more and more Christlike.)

The kingdom seems to work mysteriously, silently and not visibly expanding and making good to "grow."

13. Note 2:49–51; 8:19–21; 11:27–28.

15. Salt seasons, preserves, melts, aggravates wounds. In New Testament times it was used on the land as a form of fertilizer.

For further discussion:

1. In light of Jesus' attitude toward suffering (question 1), does He require some kind of physical or emotional masochistic martyrdom? (Note Hebrews 12:2.)

2. What did Dietrich Bonhoeffer mean by this?

Disciples are the kinds of people who take upon themselves what others would like to shake off

—The Cost of Discipleship

3. Discuss F. B. Meyer's comment:

It is quite true that whosoever will may come and take; that whosoever believeth in Him shall never perish; that the door of mercy stands open wide. But it is equally true that the faith that saves must pass such tests as these: separation, crucifixion, and renunciation.

Of renunciation he says,

If the accumulation of a life be on one scale and Christ in the other, we must choose Christ, come what may to the rest, or we must abandon our title to discipleship.

—Great Verses Through the Bible

8 / LOST OR FOUND

7–10. The older brother usually is condemned for his anger and jealousy, but he can be praised for his faithfulness. (Was he faithful for the wrong reasons?) Although the younger was extravagant, impatient, and so forth, he was penitent and humble when he clearly saw his foolishness. Neither were guiltless. The father never really condemned either son, but patiently waited or patiently explained. What a comfort!

11–12. General Background: This is often considered the most puzzling of Jesus' parables. The master commended the manager's shrewdness in protecting his future interests (his astuteness—see dictionary for definitions), not his dishonesty. Jesus makes a parallel between those who are sharp in earthly matters and those who are sharp in spiritual matters (v. 8). In verse 9 He refers to our use of money to gain friendships and thereby to protect our future spiritual interests. He seems to be saying that our generosity is eventually returned to us—in this life or the next.

In light of verses 10–13, it seems Jesus cannot be advocating the use of money for meeting self-serving material needs. After all, in verse 9 He speaks of the money eventually being gone.

13–14. The Old Testament Law did make provision for a man to divorce his wife (Deuteronomy 24:1), and in Jesus' time this "loophole" was liberally interpreted and freely exercised; men divorced their wives for little or no reason. (Women did not have this option available to them.) Jesus called for a return to the demands and spirit of the Law.

15. It may seem as if the man had been condemned for being rich, but was not Abraham himself wealthy? More likely he was condemned for having ignored Lazarus and for ignoring the teaching of the Scriptures.

16. In *Interpreting the Parables*, A. M. Hunter has paraphrased Jesus by saying,

If a man cannot be humane with the Old Testament in his hand and Lazarus on his doorstep, nothing—neither a visitant from the other world nor a revelation of the horrors of Hell—will teach him otherwise.

Closing: You may want to wrap up your session by singing the first verse of "Amazing Grace."

For further discussion:

1. Luke 16:15 is tough medicine to swallow. Who doesn't want to be fashionable (in lifestyle, in business practices, in intellectual pursuits)? Is Jesus saying that we have to shun the latest craze just because it is "highly valued"? What is He saying?

2. Women are often afraid to minister to the poor. Sometimes we even must admit, "I don't know any poor." Discuss various proposals that would, over a six-month period, lead you toward a more personal involvement in the lives of those in your local area who struggle with the bare necessities of life.

9 / MAKING CHOICES

5. What a mandate—to forgive and forgive. "Increase our faith" sounds something akin to a rather desperate "God help us." And Jesus, in turn, gives His disciples immeasurable encouragement. The smallest amount of faith will, with God's help, grow into the greatest miracles. If we, in our own strength, find forgiveness impossible, might our taking a tiny step in that direction allow the Holy Spirit to increase the effects of our faith?

8. As in the parable of the Good Samaritan, Jesus points out the true righteousness of the outcast—the one who (it was thought) could not possibly be worthy of God's grace or be considered godly. We mustn't forget that we who are Gentiles would be among this group. What groups would we tend to exclude from all the benefits of God's grace? (See Galatians 3:28.) Christ broke through any Old Testament "exclusiveness" to put all on an equal plane.

9. General Background: In verse 21 the Greek is not clear. Jesus may have meant *within* or *among*. The differences in meaning, of course, are great. *Within* would imply that the kingdom is within our hearts and not able to be seen; *among* would imply that Jesus' presence in their midst was the kingdom come, but that He was not recognized as such.

11. Again it seems that God will choose us as much as we will choose Him. Our looking to the coming Christ (as opposed to looking back like Lot's wife at what is ours) is coupled with "one will be taken," as if Christ will do the taking away.

13. Persistence will not go unnoticed. Humility and repentance—brokenness before God—is valued. We must approach God persistently, with humility and repentant hearts—aware of our bent to sin—and as a child, full of blind faith in a Father who can do anything and everything.

14. What an easy trap to fall into—comparing our righteousness to someone else's and succumbing to spiritual pride.

For further discussion:

1. Gratitude doesn't grow from nothing. What specific actions can we take to nurture gratitude in ourselves?

2. Delve deeper into what it means to enter the kingdom as a child.

3. What if we are persistent in asking God for something that is not in God's will? How might our humility and childlike trust in Him be important in this instance?

10 / ACKNOWLEDGING THE LORD

4. Jesus seems to reward as does a corporation—more work or responsibility is the reward for good work. You might refer back to 16:10—"Whoever can be trusted with very little can also be trusted with much."

5–6. What might the mina represent? Probably not money, but worth of a more spiritual nature: wisdom, understanding, talents, various Christian virtues.

7. The donkey's owners; the crowd of His followers; potentially the stones.

9. They offered their valued material possessions as a carpet for Him to walk on; they verbally declared their praises and expressed their joy.

15. Again we become aware that Jesus sees through all our tricks; we may deceive others, but not Him. He responded to the "spies' " true motives and intent rather than clearly answered their questions for which they really didn't want answers anyway.

For further discussion:

1. Discuss the following quote from Leo Tolstoy as it relates to the lordship of Christ in our lives:

Everybody thinks of changing humanity and nobody thinks of changing himself.

2. Is it possible to respond to God by saying, "No, Lord"? Or does one word completely counteract the other?

11 / WHAT LIES AHEAD?

2. Such death is obviously different from life as we know it, but to Him, death is another form of life.

4. Many scholars agree that portions of this Scripture refer to the destruction of Jerusalem (note v. 20) and portions to the Second Coming (note v. 27). Instead of analyzing the "when" of specific events, let's discuss the believer's preparedness for and reaction to the events described.

6. Verse 9—He assures us that these hard times are a part of the "plan." He knows our trials.

Verse 15—He promises us His words and wisdom in court.

Verse 33—He promises that we can rely on His words as outlasting all our physical surroundings.

7. See verse 36. We can look forward to standing before Jesus, our Redeemer and Lord.

8. Remember, Judas was the keeper of the purse for Jesus and His disciples. As treasurer, he possibly was preoccupied with money and what it could (and can) buy.

9–10. God becoming man involved many such physical aspects which you might want to review—His birth, forty-day fast, healings, admonition that if we feed our hungry brothers and sisters we are feeding Him, His impending physical pain and death. Jesus commanded that we remember Him by eating and drinking—actions that remind us of the physicalness of His life and death. The wine and bread are seeable, touchable signs of His presence among us.

You might ask the women to try to imagine how much harder remembering Christ's redeeming death would be if they only relied on prayer, meditation, and Scripture—and not on Communion.

It can be no happenstance that the verses preceding and immediately following the Last Supper are descriptions of hard times. Jesus is providing us with another means of strength—a physical one. Note that 1 Corinthians 11:26 says we are to do this until He comes again.

For further discussion:

1. How does a physical remembrance of a loved one give you strength in his or her absence?

2. Why must we guard against confusing the remembrance with the actual living person?

3. In asking us to partake of His body and blood, is Jesus asking us to partake of His sufferings? (Tradition says that ten of the twelve disciples were martyred.) Discuss this in light of C. S. Lewis's remarks:

I do not know and can't imagine what the disciples understood Our Lord to mean when, His body still unbroken and His blood unshed, He handed them the bread and wine, saying *they* were His body and blood. . . . The Command, after all, was Take, eat: not Take, understand.

—*Letters to Malcolm: Chiefly on Prayer*

12 / WERE YOU THERE?

5. In his book *Not My Will*, Andrew Murray proposes four lessons for learning to accept God's will.

1. When you are tried or afflicted, remind yourself immediately: *I am here by God's will, exactly where He planned I should be.* . . . 2. Then you may also confidently and boldly say, *"God, having brought me into this difficulty, will surely give me the grace to conduct myself in it as I ought."* . . . 3. You may go even farther and say, *"God Himself will teach me why He brought me into this trial."* . . . 4. Then you will also dare to say, *"God's will, which brought me here, can also bring me out of my troubles, at His own time and in His own way."*

7. He may be saying something as simple as "Hard times are coming. I am leaving you to your own resources." (Remember the Holy Spirit would not descend on the disciples, giving them power, until Pentecost, over a month away.) He could have been telling them to ready themselves for emotional and spiritual battle (a command similar to "Gird up your loins") and to be ready to face, although not participate in, violence that is prompted by the kingdom.

The phrase "that is enough" in verse 38 is not saying "two swords are enough," but rather "enough, already" to cut off their talk of "nonsense."

8. Judas's moves were premeditated and calculated. Peter, in sincerity, had stated his loyalty and, in the end, seemed motivated by fear rather than by malice. This in no way excuses Peter's fear or denial. Sin is sin. In 22:32 Jesus tells Peter what good should come of his denial and repentance. Matthew 27:1–10 tells of the destructive end of Judas's remorse. Note 2 Corinthians 7:10 for further insight.

10. He carried your sins and mine to the grave, paying the blood sacrifice necessary for our reconciliation with God.

12. Jesus' mere acknowledgment of them and the way His concern for them took precedence over His concern for Himself is a consolation. Imagine yourself enduring His physical pain. Would you have even noticed the people around you?

14, 15. Ask the group to try to identify with the humility of the cross. Jesus knew He was innocent; He knew He was capable of stepping down. He carried for a few hours all the physical and emotional pain of world history, yet it was a willing and conscious sacrifice made for each of us, even for His enemies and those who hated Him. We might not be guilty of a martyr complex if we are suffering for our children, but for our enemies?

For further discussion:

1. Discuss whether or not Judas would have been forgiven if, in the second before his death, he had truly repented.

2. Who was responsible for Jesus' death? Were *you* there?

13 / SPREAD THE WORD!

1. The tragedy of the day was made obvious in the sky. In 22:53 Jesus said that this was the reign of darkness. Satan had managed to kill the Son of God. But God's plan is bigger than Satan's. Jesus' sacrifice of His life as atonement for sin tore down the barrier between God and us.

6, 7. Seeing was believing. In Mark 16:14 Jesus rebuked the disciples for this trait. Remember Jesus had told them that the resurrection would happen, and still they believed only when they saw with their own eyes. Their belief had little to do with faith, only with sight. Our faith is just that—faith, as Jesus' life as man on earth was confined to first-century Palestine.

13. Note Matthew 28:20, where Jesus made His presence in absence even more clear. The disciples now obviously understood Jesus' spiritual power and, although they might not have known exactly what the presence of the Holy Spirit would mean for them, they trusted that He would somehow make Jesus' presence near.

For further discussion:

Discuss the following quote of Andrew Murray:

Only he who gives himself wholeheartedly to do God's will, desiring the indwelling of Christ for that purpose, can fully experience Christ in his heart and can truly say, 'Christ liveth in me.' On the other hand, only he who can honestly say, 'Christ liveth in me,' is able to do the will of God always and with joy.

—*Not My Will*